WI	AB	DI	
5	7	10	18	2	20	

G000291861

Witney Library
Welch Way
Witney
Oxon OX28 6JH

Tel: 01993 703659

DIDCOT
OX11 8RU
TEL. 01235 813103

ABINGDON LIBRARY
The Charter, Abingdon
Tel. 01235 520374

To renew this book, phone 0845 1202811 or visit
our website at www.libcat.oxfordshire.gov.uk
You will need your library PIN number
(available from your library)

**OXFORDSHIRE
COUNTY COUNCIL**
SOCIAL & COMMUNITY SERVICES
www.oxfordshire.gov.uk

3303280786

Selima Hill grew up in a family of painters on farms in England and Wales, and has lived by the sea in Dorset for over 30 years. She received a Cholmondeley Award in 1986, and was a Royal Literary Fund Fellow at Exeter University in 2003-06. She won first prize in the Arvon/*Observer* International Poetry Competition with part of *The Accumulation of Small Acts of Kindness* (1989), one of several extended sequences in *Gloria: Selected Poems* (Bloodaxe Books, 2008). *Gloria* includes work from *Saying Hello at the Station* (1984), *My Darling Camel* (1988), *A Little Book of Meat* (1993), *Aeroplanes of the World* (1994), *Violet* (1997), *Bunny* (2001), *Portrait of My Lover as a Horse* (2002), *Lou-Lou* (2004) and *Red Roses* (2006). Her latest collections from Bloodaxe are *The Hat* (2008); *Fruitcake* (2009); *People Who Like Meatballs* (2012), shortlisted for both the Forward Poetry Prize and the Costa Poetry Award; *The Sparkling Jewel of Naturism* (2014); *Jutland* (2015), shortlisted for both the T.S. Eliot Prize and the Roehampton Poetry Prize; *The Magnitude of My Sublime Existence* (2016); and *Splash Like Jesus* (2017).

Violet was a Poetry Book Society Choice and was shortlisted for all three of the UK's major poetry prizes, the Forward Prize, T.S. Eliot Prize and Whitbread Poetry Award. *Bunny* won the Whitbread Poetry Award, was a Poetry Book Society Choice, and was shortlisted for the T.S. Eliot Prize. *Lou-Lou* and *The Hat* were Poetry Book Society Recommendations, while *Jutland* was a Special Commendation.

SELIMA HILL

SPLASH LIKE JESUS

BLOODAXE BOOKS

Copyright © Selima Hill 2017

ISBN: 978 1 78037 349 2

First published 2016 by
Bloodaxe Books Ltd,
Eastburn,
South Park,
Hexham,
Northumberland NE46 1BS.

www.bloodaxebooks.com
For further information about Bloodaxe titles
please visit our website or write to
the above address for a catalogue.

Supported by
**ARTS COUNCIL
ENGLAND**

LEGAL NOTICE

All rights reserved. N
reproduced, stored in
transmitted in any for
mechanical, photocop
without prior written

Requests to publish v
must be sent to Bloo

Selima Hill has assert
Section 77 of the Co
to be identified as the

OXFORDSHIRE LIBRARY SERVICE	
3303280786	
Askews & Holts	04-May-2017
821.92	£12.00

Cover design: Neil Astley & Pamela Robertson-Pearce.

Printed in Great Britain by Bell & Bain Limited, Glasgow, Scotland, on
acid-free paper sourced from mills with FSC chain of custody certification.

CONTENTS

Buttercup the Sloth

Lobo-Lobo

Behold My Father on His Bicycle

BUTTERCUP THE SLOTH

How can they not revere what I revere? How is it that
my gods are invisible to them? It's inexcusable…

GORDON LISH (in conversation)

PART ONE

THE LETTER

Mothers

Never underestimate how strange they are
and just how strange being strange can be –

the way they're never wrong, for example;
the way they say – the way *my mother* says –

never go, or even think of going,
anywhere near a Great Dane.

The Frantic Hens

No one really knows what she likes,
or even who she is; for example,

everybody calls her something different.
I myself don't call her anything.

In that way my mother is like God.
The frantic hens, however, can't wait

to hear the new exotic names I'm giving them
they'll never know will make them look ridiculous.

Easter at My Grandmother's

My mother is reluctantly but carefully
hiding chocolate eggs in the drawing room –

exhausted by not letting go of sorrow
and by resisting joy, what joy there is…

The cook is always very bad-tempered.
The one-legged goose is bad-tempered too.

But if you think I'm going to say my mother is –
nothing could be further from the truth!

Kittens

The newborn kittens frighten her – like bees
that bump against her ankles in a rage

because they think she won't give back their wings.
They frighten her so much she won't come in.

Tiger-moths

She tells me I must never touch the Tiger-moths
and certainly not the Woolly Bears

that rub against my fingers like warm buns –
and everybody likes warm buns.

Never Be Alone with a Goose

Never be alone with a goose.
Never look a stranger in the eye.
Never get undressed near a window
and never ask to stroke a Great Dane.

Never wear a hat to feed the chickens.
Never start a book and not finish it.
Never go upstairs empty-handed
and only buy a blazer that's too big.

Always draw the curtains. Other families
celebrate birthdays: we don't.
Photographs aren't necessary either.
And telephones only make one cry.

My Mother and the Yachtsmen

I hear the booming voices of the yachtsmen
and see the flash of lipstick and red nails.

If I wait long enough a hand
will toss a bag of crisps into the dark.

I know that I myself never hold,
and never will, anything against her.

I Disagree with Everything She Says

I disagree with everything she says.
Never laugh in public, for example.

Never wear white socks. Or whip cream.
And, if you are a girl, which I am,

never ride a horse – but I can,
if the sun is very hot, wear shorts!

(With the shorts, I have to wear boots,
kneelength boots, because of the snakes.)

Mrs M.

Of all the mothers who are not my mother,
none is so much fun as Mrs M.,

whose wrinkles she and I measure daily:
she's got the body of a red Shar-Pei!

Jam

If it knows I'm here, which it will do,
no amount of jam will placate it

and all its greedy friends will taxi in
and sting me on the lips until I die

unless I know the answer – which is mud.
And never wear yellow to a picnic.

The Tin Containing Butterdrops

If I help her wash and dry the eggs
she reaches for the tin containing butterdrops

but Mrs P. can no more be my mother
than Cyclops the mother of a bicycle.

Fairy Liquid

Even rats and guinea-pigs have names
but not my mother, she is too thin,

she doesn't even like being looked at.
What she really likes is Fairy Liquid.

Armbands

Although I'm much too old to wear armbands
she's waving them about like a maniac,

her panic-stricken eyes as pink as pimples
those with pimples are compelled to squeeze.

Garages Make Me Feel Sick

Did I ever tell you she loves driving?
At least I think she does. It's hard to tell.

She certainly likes looking at roadmaps,
mostly with the man at the garage.

It's boring to be helpful and anyway
garages make me feel sick.

Mrs P.

Everyone agrees she's much too fat
but all she does is eat all the more

until the day I find her on her lounger
with a fly crawling up her nose

which scares not only me but the dog
my mother says is nothing but *imaginary*.

Glass

Unfortunately other people's mothers
know the words of all my favourite songs
and sing them at the top of their voices
until they laugh so much they've got to stop

and stuff themselves with chocolate but my mother
is like a mother made of spun glass:
she rustles like a bird with spun-glass tail-feathers.
And (did I say?) her waist-long hair is *silver*!

Zoo

I'm not complaining, I just think it's odd
to never take your daughter to the zoo
nor, even in a heatwave, to the lido
or *lido* or however you pronounce it
or anywhere public like that.

Red Ants

If she doesn't rest after lunch
her beautiful white face and white bones –

and don't forget how elegant she was –
will turn into a little heap of sugar-grains

and ants will come from far and wide with wheelbarrows
attracted by the sugar even ants

will find, to their surprise, is much too sweet;
and, all too soon, they become enraged

and argue with each other till the sugar,
once so white, is speckled with red limbs.

The Letter

It's summertime, just me and my dog,
and when we get too bored in the kitchen
we run outside – where we see my mother
standing at the end of the garden
staring at a letter, with her back to us;

and then she turns, still holding the letter,
and walks straight past, as if she doesn't know me,
and never will again, because, alas,
those who see, or think they see, their mother
crying in the garden will be shot.

PART TWO

SUNNYSIDE

The Clock

She never moves without a large clock
because she is convinced – don't ask me why –

that, if she doesn't time me, I will drown,
and, even if she does, she thinks I will –

right in front of where she's now sitting
and where she has been sitting *since the beginning*,

watching me excavate my moats
in which a woman with a clock is drowning.

Centipede

From where I'm hiding in the long grass
like a clockwork centipede whose key

God has either lost or pretends He has,
I can see my mother and she's crying.

Everything Is Coming Together

Everything is coming together
or, in other words, going wrong,

and, if it isn't going wrong now,
it will be in a minute, as the sea

holds me in its arms, and as I realise
being scared is how I want to be.

How to Lay Eggs

When I say I've seen the Easter Bunnies
with kayaks full of eggs come ashore

she says that rabbits, even chocolate ones,
can't, however hard they try, lay eggs;

she says that many thousands have perished
trying to work it out but they can't.

Coconut

Buttercup just hangs there, either smiling
or almost smiling. She expects nothing.
She's given up trying to be a cow
or wanting to be free and so she knows
she'll never be discouraged – on the contrary,
she's given up trying to be discouraged!
She'll hang up upside-down like this quite happily

for several hours and doesn't mind a bit
looking like an elongated coconut
or being called by someone else's name.
And by the way it's not as if I think
it's clever to be indolent – I don't –
all I'm saying is: please God,
may my mother be a bit more carefree!

The Hunt

I can't remember now what they call them
but there they are, on the far horizon,

disappearing off at top speed,
leaving the exhausted-looking hunters

standing on their knoll, feeling faint;
while hardy ones still peer through the binoculars

they tell each other never to forget;
who, if I run away, will hunt me down.

The Queen

When at last I creep from my hiding place
everyone has gone. It's getting dark.

In my mother's bedroom where a fly
throws itself against a window-pane

I see a pile of letters by the bed
and a pill box. For a long time

I stand and listen to the only sound:
the fly, my subject, over whom I reign.

Surrender, Surrender

Why do I always have to be so difficult?
So someone has to take me somewhere else

so she can have her precious 'rest' at last?
And stare uninterrupted at the mist

gathering like sheep against her window-pane
as if to say *surrender, surrender* –

but my mother has her own ideas
and these ideas do not include surrender.

Tinny Cows

Athletic, chaste, alone and disobedient,
I run ahead, way ahead, and leave her

waiting for our lunches to be ready –
apples, Spam, tomatoes, stale cake

and tiny cubes of cheese where tinny cows
try in vain to moo, but they are dumb

and never say, or even whisper, anything,
in spite of their spectacular earrings.

Songbird

Back and forth she goes like a songbird
who finds she's got a cuckoo in her nest
and doesn't know how not to go on feeding it

although the cuckoo only gets more vicious,
the songbird more bewildered, till at last
the so-called songbird loses her song.

Boxes

My mother is so frightened of the cats
that sleep all day upstairs in cardboard boxes

dreaming of the blood of wounded wrens,
I think she's even frightened of the boxes.

Pig Farming

Has she brought us here because of me?
After all, she's cold, she's got no friends.
and nothing else to do but read her flower book,
or perch herself above the waves and draw.
She must be hating every minute of it –
the dogs, the Spam, the toffee-coloured bedroom,
and, worst of all, the budgies, specially trained
to kiss you on the lips. This is grim.

My mother hides upstairs in the bathroom
trying not to touch anything.
Outside in the mud, rotting beet.
I've had my first experience of pig farming
and Coconut Delight – and of surfing,
which God, because He loves me, has laid on for me.
By 'loves', I don't mean 'pities'. He just knows
I'll be bowled over by His ingenuity.

The Decline and Fall of the Roman Empire in Hardback

My mother's always reading, or, not reading,
but carrying about, a large volume
of Gibbon's *Decline and Fall of the Roman Empire*:
God has somehow even thought of that!
Not only the Roman Empire, from start to finish,
but also Edward Gibbon, so that mothers
can read about it on their holidays.

Summer Nights

My mother's never seen me when I'm happy.
She's never seen me dance, for example,
and never chased a wolf across the dunes.

Of course she does come out when it's warm
but only to sit quietly on the terrace
waiting for us all to come home,

which makes the sweetness of the summer nights,
of running through the pinewoods in our shorts
calling *Lobo! Lobo!*, less sweet.

Honey

I run outside with honey on my arms
and wait for wasps and when they've all arrived

I wave to her in my new wasp-jacket –
a woman who was never known to smile.

Buckets

Not only does my mother fear kittens
but also buckets and the sound of buckets

because a bucket might contain a kitten
and, even more than kittens, she fears drowning.

I Contradict Everything She Says

I contradict everything she says
till in the end she never says anything

and dust and dust-mites occupy her air-ways
so, even if she wants to, she can't.

Swimming in the Dark

My mother is afraid of many things
but think how brave she must have had to be

to face the girl the Rhadamanthine 'Head'
has 'had no option but to expel'!

PART THREE

SUGAR

Sugar

I follow them at night to upstairs rooms
then run for it – abandoning my victim

to cups of coffee made with so much sugar
the coffee cups and mattresses are sticky with it.

The Eyelashes of Ostriches

I want to tell you all about the manes,
or not so much the manes as the hands

that grip the manes, and have this strange effect on me,
that isn't love (love for whom? for what?)

or, if it is, it is but it's impossible,
like a rock for another rock.

(By the way, the eyelashes of ostriches
are made of feathers, not of hairs, like ours.)

God Has Thought of Everything

Nipples, woolly mammoths, circumcision,
God has thought of everything – except

how to uninvent things: as things stand
everything can never not have happened.

Ostriches

I'll write about anything from ostriches –
whose kick can kill you if you get too close –

to mothers, and my mother in particular,
who stays downstairs trying not to think about it.

Rodeo

My mother is afraid of everything,
everything, that is, to do with me –

and now I'm off to ride the wild pony
we've all agreed I'm not allowed to ride.

She looks at me and bursts into tears
which trickle down her cheeks and down her neck

and round the tiny pearls of her necklace
which quiver in response to their nudges.

When Darkness Falls

When darkness falls, I take my swimming things
and make my way alone to the sea

that whispers in the ears of angry daughters
what can't be said by mothers on dry land.

Eerie Bittern

The eerie bittern – this may sound unfair –
spends her days pretending to be reeds

and people think she's sulking, but she's not,
she's like my mother: sunlight gives her headaches.

The Bearded Man

Never be alone on a boat
and never be alone with a man

because a man is *sexually arousing*
and sexual arousal is disturbing,

either for the man or for you
or, if he is a bearded man, for both of you.

Monster Cloud Formations

She likes to bowl along an open road
which I do nothing but complain about

but she herself adores – as the sky
on windy nights adores its monster cloud formations.

The Knife

Never be alone with a knife
and never be alone with a woman
who's wielding a knife and, God forbid,
if that woman is your own mother
then you'll know something's very wrong;

and why are her hands so cold, and her eyes so small?
And where has she been, and why is she holding the knife
she knows she needs to hide from the guard
because, although she knows the guard's imaginary,
the knife he wants to save me from is real.

Fish

One woman who, in a way, supports me –
by shouting at my mother day and night
about the way she should or shouldn't treat me –
is someone, sadly, whom I do not trust,
who shouts at you so loudly she leaves you

feeling sick, like a sick bird
waiting in the mud to be saved
though how she will be saved and from what
the pea-brained bird's too sick to understand.
All her brain can understand is fish.

Miss T.

Every time she punishes my sins,
after several days she will apologise

because, she says, she wants me to know
that she herself's *my greatest admirer*.

Virginity

Although I find cake extremely boring,
it's nowhere near as boring as virginity,

virginity *according to my mother*,
which, as virgins know, does not work.

The Gold Handbag

I'm sitting in a field like a cow
minding my own business when a man

totters past with a gold handbag,
as if to reassure himself of something.

(When I say 'minding my own business'
what I mean is dreaming of Great Danes,

white ones, with irregular patches,
black or blue, preferably blue.)

Ratbag

Why can't I have a Miniature Wire-haired Dachshund?
And why can't I have a Harlequin Great Dane?

And who is calling who *an old ratbag*?
And anyway what is an old ratbag?

And what is being 'excited', on the one hand,
and being *'over-excited'* on the other?

And where does everything come from in the first place –
the sun, the moon, the stars, the shimmering lake?

And all the mothers and all the mothers' daughters,
the lovely ones, the not so lovely ones,

the ones who live, or should that be, who crawl
on their knees among the millipedes?

Where do we all come from? We don't know.
But luckily it really doesn't matter.

Lily

It's got to just arise, like the lily,
but when it doesn't I just run away

because I'm simply not the sort of person
to settle imperturbably in mud.

Chomsky

I wish I was a dog with a choc ice
that somebody will have bought for me;

I also wish – unlikely, I know –
that somebody will have called me Chomsky.

The Violinists and the Viola Players

The only girls approved by the Management –
the violinists and the viola players

whose straightened hair and hairless arms and legs
I myself am much too proud to marvel at –

shut themselves away in distant cubby-holes
with neither food nor drink for so long

no one knows until it's far too late
the lovely girls have turned into flies.

My Mother at the Station

She checks her scarf, or what she calls her 'headscarf'
and what she calls her 'purse' – the old handbag

that lives beside her on the front seat –
and powders her long nose and then her chin.

She's here to meet her daughter. I.e. me.
She thinks *She should be here any minute*.

PART FOUR

SWIMMING CHICKENS

Swimming Chickens

Is everyone who's fat a bit thick?
And is it true that oligarchs masturbate

more than normal men and women do?
that apricots 'work well' with mayonnaise;

that ugliness lasts longer than beauty:
that helping people is a waste of time?

And how do chickens swim and do I smell
and is the key to happiness less sex

and why are newborn babies not like syrup
and just because a question is a question

it doesn't mean to say that there's an answer
(it's just its little trick to make you think there is!) –

and yes, there's more to life than punctuation,
such as being forthright, like the waves.

Tennis with My Mother

My mother disapproves of nearly everything,
of Lucozade, chihuahuas, even hope

because she knows we've got to hope for something
but what that something is she can't work out...

(it's true it's just a guess about chihuahuas –
I'm sure she's never seen one in her life –

but the word *chihuahua* sounds so cheery
I squeeze it in wherever I can!)

Radish

I had a dog she never liked called Radish.
She never even touched her. Did you know

the man who shot the students on Utøya
shot them 'out of love'? Because he loved us?

And wanted to protect us? Did you know
that those of us who fail to use violence,

as he had had to do, have betrayed him?
And did you know, on Kirkeveien, in Oslo,

his tag can still be seen? That his mother
was told to leave his food outside his door

in order not to risk, or to reduce the risk,
of her, a woman, being smelled by him?

But what I really want to say is this:
Radish loved my mother all the same.

Mrs L.

Every night she comes and sits beside me
and watches me but she says nothing.

I live here while I study Ancient Greek,
nothing else, to the highest possible standard.

Psychiatrists

Psychiatrists can be of either gender:
never be alone with a man

and never be alone with a woman.
And never climb on or into laps.

The Hospital

I know my mother never comes near it
(she's quite distraught enough as it is)

but late at night I sometimes catch a glimpse of her
riding in an ostrich-drawn sedan

along the sweeping drive below my window
and past the moonlit nurseries where the ostrich-babies

are fed on rabbit droppings and old nails,
but it isn't possible to wave.

Sister

She looks as if her eyes will pop out
and scares the other patients till they wet themselves
– idiots! She doesn't scare me.

I like the fact the fact that I'm unbearable
is fine by her and I like the tightness –
so tight she can't sit down – of her uniform.

My Mother's Devotion

She does what is expected of her but
she doesn't seem to dare to do more

and little does she know I'm trying to say
how brave I think she is and how devoted

because it isn't easy to devote yourself
to somebody you can't understand.

My Only Suitor

She tries her best not to hate anything
although she doesn't always succeed –

she hates all cats and kittens, for example,
and later she will hate my only suitor.

My Mother's Car

She may have been happy. I don't know.
She doesn't seem very happy now
and talking on the phone just upsets her –

but don't forget my mother did love something:
she loved her car, and everything about it,
and everyone would wave as she flew by.

The Key to Happiness

My mother – this may sound unkind – my mother
doesn't seem to know if she will ever

find the key to Happiness again –
which makes me think she should have been a wasp:

a wasp is very good at being a wasp
and never loses, far less misses, anything!

Tender Mice

My mother is not only my mother
but also someone else altogether,
another woman, I can see that now,
who isn't, and will never be, invited
to live with us, downstairs, in the present;
who lives alone upstairs in the past,
who can't stand up, whose tiny heart is breaking;

the room is hot, and bands of tender mice
come pouring in until she can't move;
they pile on her legs and on her lap:
she drowns in mice, right up to her chin;
aghast, in her disintegrating dress,
she's trying to remember who she is,
and, when she does, trying to forget.

Home

Perhaps I shouldn't say this but my mother
appears to me to be like a child

nobody knows how to comfort
or how, or even whether, to home.

Flower

We are not the same. On the contrary
we are very different, as you know.

She is very beautiful: I'm not.
She is shy: I am rather fierce.

Being shy, she acts in a shy way.
Being fierce, I act in a fierce way.

I'm like a dye or a stain:
she is like a transient cut flower.

Dog

Never live at home with your mother
and never ask your mother for a dog

and if you never ask you never get
and, if you do, you never get either!

Husbands

How can I explain to my mother
that, now I can decide for myself,
I've realised I don't want one after all?
That I'd rather have a Great Dane instead?

Preferably a Harlequin, its patch
as blue as Danish blue and asymmetrical,
or possibly a Boston. One last thing –
the way the ears hang down like warm catalpa beans

makes me wish I too had ears like that,
with lots of room to hang my earrings on,
and lots of velvet folds for friends to fondle.
Anyway at least I don't drool.

Breath

Imagine being overrun by dust-mites,
especially by the faeces of dust-mites;

imagine my warm breath on your cheek;
imagine being *too close to me*.

Snowball

She always says *Oh darling, you're so kind*
even when I'm not being kind.
And then she'll go to sleep – like a snowball
leaving for its home in the snow.

(I want to say more about kindness;
and also to explain what happens next;
somehow to explain how, if you hold it,
the less of it you find there is to hold –

but what's the point of trying to explain it
when even to describe it is beyond me –
the hospital, the pain, the frosted windows,
the long, gloved fingers trying to find a vein?)

LOBO-LOBO

It is easy for a bird to hurt a horse whose back is broken.

CHINESE PROVERB

Ankle Socks

Why do they always have to wear white ankle socks?
And why do they always have to smell of bubble-bath?

And why do I always have to have so many?
Doesn't God love me any more?

The Person with the Red Suitcase

Yes, the person with the red suitcase
(although it isn't red, it's more like *apricot*;

and nor is it a suitcase, it's a *vanity-case*,
it's even got the mirror on the lid)

the person is myself, whom my sisters
want to wrest my little suitcase from.

It's like a pug with an orange handle
and cheers me up. Or like a prisoner's ant.

Giants

They're standing in the rain in the dark
like giants with no heads except mouths

shouting at each other in a language
I refuse to want to understand

and I refuse to fear the giant shadows
that billow with no heads against the walls.

My Sisters' Little Sister

My sisters know *only too well*
that I, their little sister, am adorable.

They want to see me take my little suitcase
and hit the road and never come back.

The Centre of the Universe

They think they are the *centre of the universe*
whereas in fact I am. So you see

either we all fight like cat and dog
or I have the sense to ignore them

and let them fight themselves, which they do.
They do it all the time so they're used to it.

Goldfish

The goldfish, nibbling bubbles like my sisters
nibbling their Ryvita, seem to like me,

or anyway my fingertips; my sisters
have never even noticed my fingertips.

Dressed Echidna

I may not be the sweetest little girl,
in fact I must be much the most unlikable,
with my woolly hair and scarred head
that no one wants to look at, far less touch;
I'm not the most attractive, I admit,
and what I really like to do is sulk.

My sisters are too dumb, and not worth talking to –
too dumb to know what *dressed echidna* is,
or whose last words were *Spray the peonies*,
or what a *need-to-know* basis is;
too dumb to be afraid of serial killers.
I sulk because I'm disappointed in them.

Rowley

My sisters have been sent to various boarding-schools
where they have learnt to pray if nothing else;

they pray and pray but it makes no difference,
the holidays still stink of me and Rowley.

Snow

You can't just stand there all by yourself,
my sisters say, and jab me in the ribs,
while outside in the dark it starts to snow

and everything we love will be buried
and nobody and nothing will be saved.
Move, they're saying, *move, you selfish cow.*

My Baby

The deal is if he lets me carry him
I promise to protect him. When my sisters

swing him round their heads by his lock
I promise I will reinforce the studs;

when they drizzle honey down his hinges
I'll wash him for as long as it takes.

Pug

He's like a little pug, which is a dog,
and feels light but at the same time *springy* –

as if it doesn't matter anymore
what the difference is between Emptiness

and Nothingness and nothing – and the handle
is warm and polished like a ping-pong paddle's.

Unexpected Booms of Cassowaries

Although I know the truth about 'table tennis'
I'm going to call it 'ping-pong' because *ping-pong*

sounds like what it is; like the *booms*
in 'unexpected booms of cassowaries' do.

My Sisters in Their Cowboy Hats

They stride into the kitchen in their cowboy hats
and look at me as if I'm not there.

On days like this I hate them all: my sisters
couldn't care less about the swimming-pools.

Don't You Dare Open My Door

Don't you dare open my door
and don't you dare touch my little suitcase

and don't you dare lie to me because
nothing you can do will appease me.

Our Lonely House

Their crying is so pitiful I'm scared
although of course I never say I am;

all I do is tell them to SHUT UP
and throw things at them – porridge, buckets, anything –

and anyone walking past the house
would think we're mad, but no one does walk past.

Dogs Are Not Allowed in the Drawing-room

Dogs are not allowed in the drawing-room
so why is there a dog on the sofa?

Sprawling like a dog who thinks it owns the place?
Or, rather, like a dog who's so enlightened

it doesn't need to think or own anything;
who, free from thinking, free from owning, sleeps

upside down on other people's sofas
while effortlessly giving rise to chaos.

Arson

Can an arsonist be a girl?
A girl who has herself been badly burnt?

Who runs towards the forest late at night
with eyes the size of persimmons and tennis balls?

Or would the girl be better off in bed,
seeing as it's late, and school tomorrow?

The Violinists

No one ever calls the hens bad mothers
for failing to remember all the eggs

and no one ever calls my sisters slackers:
they call them *virtuosi* instead.

The World's Deepest Lake

I'm lying on the sofa like a fish
that's being screamed at till it can't move,

or maybe it still can, but it won't,
it won't be doing any more flapping

but prays to God to send it Lake Baikal,
if Lake Baikal's the world's deepest lake,

and, even if it's not, to send it anyway,
or anything, it begs, that's not dry land.

Lobo-Lobo

Everybody knows that men in uniform
are suffering from low self-esteem;

that those of us who've got a sweet tooth
need to eat lots and lots of chocolate

or else we lose our temper; Texas Longhorns
never wear anything but orange;

the human race is obviously progressing;
gastropods are always inconsolable;

that all these handmade chocolates cost a fortune,
that someone should have thought of that before;

that thongs are unhygienic and that kindness
is better left to somebody else –

and everybody knows, and abides by,
the rules of Lobo-Lobo except me.

If a Clock

If a clock is trying not to tick
it's going to get upset, because it can't;

if a clock wants to think, it can't,
it's got to wait until it winds down.

The Dolls

I make them do exactly what I want.
I sit them down in knitted frocks like dolls

who beg me to forgive them – and I do!
I finally forgive them! Only joking.

They Hate the Cold

They hate the cold, they hate getting wet,
they hate the mud, the cows, the yellow cow-pats,

they hate the thought of crayfish down their ears,
of damselflies entangled in their hair-dos;

they hate the splashing coots that splash like Jesus
if Jesus had enormous feet like coots

but most of all my sisters hate me,
bursting in with armfuls of wet swimming-things.

The Earwigs Are Distraught

My sisters have been bringing in the windfalls
and leaving them around to trip me up

and now the kitchen's overrun with earwigs
determined not to show how scared they are

whereas in fact the earwigs are distraught
and here and there you see them on high ledges

contemplating *ending it all*:
you see them teeter as they live again

the happy days they spent digesting rose-petals,
inside the nooks and crannies they called home.

My Almond Snowman Cake

I'm holed up in my bedroom like a cat
that spends the night on tiptoe hunting rats;

that will not tolerate imperfection;
that's grieving like the last cat in the world:

my sisters have defaced my almond snowman cake
and I *never want to see them again!*

Ginger Cookies

Ginger *cookies*? Ginger *biscuits*? Which?
How can they not know? Or even want to know?

And how can they so casually refer to
the keyring with the Leonberger on it

as 'the keyring with the Belgian Shepherd on it'?
How can they not care about the schwa?

Vinyl. Postman. Harmony. My sisters
when they see me coming see nothing.

Only in Their Dreams

O, too much sex has brought them to their knees
and every room has got its curtains drawn!

(By 'too much sex' I think you know I mean
too much sex but *only in their dreams* –

dreams that have reduced them all to screaming,
to screaming till they crawl upstairs, defeated,

while everybody else is acting normal
and everywhere you go stinks of coffeepots.)

They Want Meringues

They want meringues, they want double cream;
they want a man, a shop, the mall itself;

they want the Hand of God – but most of all
they want my little suitcase to come home to.

Being Friends or Not Being Friends

Being friends is out of the question –
or 'being friends' according to my sisters,

which I myself feel nothing but disdain for:
I never listen to a word they say.

My Sisters' Nostrils

What annoys me most is the nostrils
they wouldn't dream of piercing; mine, however,

are like the jam-jar lids they stab with skewers
to make their nasty jam-jar wasp-traps with.

My Sisters' Noses

I can make their noses much too big
and I can make their breasts the size of peas

and I can drag them off to somewhere hot
and wrap them round the necks of yellow tigers

and make them kick and scream until they faint
and finally fall silent, but I mustn't.

The Fish on the Sofa

I'm lying on the sofa like a fish
whose face is full of fish hooks being screamed at

until the people screaming all turn blue
and the fish they're screaming at stops moving.

My Sisters' Hair

My sisters are obsessed with their hair
and scream if it goes wrong whereas I
cultivate equanimity,

or what the doctor calls 'equinamity',
which may or may not be his way of teasing me
because he knows I always get things right.

A Game of Telegrams

Everyone is gathered in the drawing-room
with books and breadboards balanced on their knees
waiting for the game to get started

but one of my sisters keeps on asking
if the word is 'teaDRESS' or 'teaDRESSES'
and then ignoring what I say: teaDRESSES.

Honey

I never lift a finger. Why would I?
They moan at me whatever I do.

Once I dripped honey in their handbags
but otherwise I mostly just sit here.

Angels from the Realms of Glory

My sisters are the size and shape of angels
if angels were to wear expensive bras

and shoes that can't be flown in; who can't fly;
who walk about in hats they think are haloes;

who walk about in squashed, unceremonious
bobble-hats and cowboy hats and turbans,

turbans meaning turbans made of towels
they walk about in when they've washed their tresses;

my sisters are not sisters but angels,
angels with no wings and nylon hair –

either with no wings or wings gone wrong
which make them flop and twizzle as they fall.

Other People's Cars

My sisters' cars are crawling with ants
because my sisters have become more interested

in driving round in *other people's* cars,
preferably the kind that gleam like cough lozenges.

My Sisters' Faces

Their faces are enormous and uncouth;
their eyes, what you can see of them, are red

and quiver with a kind of frightening innocence
from underneath the scratchable ears;

their eyelashes are bristly and white;
their noses are not noses but *snouts*

that have the nerve to mutter as they oink
that it's not them it's me that's pig-headed.

As Ugly as a Shoebill

My sisters flash their skinny, snow-white legs
while telling me to *do as I am told*
and saying I'm as *ugly as a shoebill* –

but can't they understand the simple fact
I *want* to be as ugly as a shoebill?
And doing as I'm told *spoils everything*?

Blister-packs

I like to get things right – for example,
the hundreds of starlings they sucked into one of the
engines

were starlings and not sparrows. God's the same.
After all, He invented blister-packs.

Baking

My sisters like to spend the mornings baking
and tearing at each other's throats like cats.

I prefer not to bake, like Christ
Who didn't bake and Who redeemed us all.

Ponies

My sisters trot about in six-inch heels
getting on my nerves, like little ponies

dressed in frilly dresses in a pantomime
trying not to kick the plastic roses.

Going Shopping

When they reappear with all their bags,
one of them will fly into a rage,

gather up the cats and sweep upstairs.
I would never dream of going shopping.

Men

Who their father is I can't be sure
but obviously he's not Adam Faith.

Bungalow

It's taking them for ever to get ready
and when it all goes wrong they hit the roof

but, as for me, I emerge from sleep
readymade and perfect as a bungalow.

My Sisters' Necks

They're welcome to the six-inch-high high-heels
they totter up and down the High Street in

as if they're trying to break their tiny necks.
When I walk, I walk. End of story.

The Spider

I watch them like a spider watches flies
that think they've been ordained by God to buzz;

I watch them with my tiny screwed-up eyes
and if I'm feeling bored enough I pounce.

Toilet-bags

My sisters have got undulating hair,
evil pets, expensive-looking jeans,

a sister who's for ever scribbling secrets
in tiny little notebooks like a spy,

and toilet-bags they're never seen without
to hold the pills that cool their filthy tempers.

Heron

When the doctor comes into the room
I leave the table, like a tall heron

whom somebody disturbs at her lake,
somebody who is unworthy of her.

The Doctor

The doctor is enormous but mild
and when he takes his place in the dining-room

my sisters all smile and stop breathing.
(And when I say smile, I mean smirk.)

This Paradise of Love

One of my sisters, in a dressing-gown,
creeps into the kitchen with a knife

and slices several lemons for herself
and then returns the knife to her handbag –

though why she needs the lemons, or the handbag,
or even her own knife, is beyond me;

or how it is that, tragic as it sounds,
this boundlessly-bejewelled world of ours,

this *paradise of love*, is a world
she seems to have no will to enter into.

Up and Down the Stairs

Up and down the stairs in floods of tears,
scattering small dogs and priceless necklaces,

my sisters don't believe me when I humour them
because they know I don't believe myself.

What I Really Want to Do

What I really want to do is fall
but neither land nor melt, like a snowflake

that's celebrating having been a glacier
by falling for as long as it can

before it disappears; like a snowflake
that never cries nor lets itself be handled.

Dispirin

Like a sister made of Dispirin,
when my sisters scream, I dissolve.

Trombones

The tears my sisters wilfully provoke,
that trickle down their suitors' cheeks like rain

trickling down the insides of trombones,
make them feel good about themselves.

My Sisters' Cars

My sisters drive fast cars – not 'drive' exactly,
they park them in the road and leave them there

to sit and rust while apoplectic suitors
are running up impressive bills to salvage them.

Enormous Flowers Wrapped in Cellophane

My sisters like to warm the laps of men –
men who cheat, who drink, who dye their hair;

who buy, or get their secretaries to buy,
enormous flowers wrapped in Cellophane

and boxes of expensive hand-made chocolates
until the day – or usually the night! –

the smell of flowers makes everyone throw up
and chocolates will no longer be the answer.

The Snowdrop

My sisters let themselves get kicked around
by people with big mouths and big muscles

that ripple underneath their shirts like rats
to whom I am as pointless as a snowdrop.

My Sisters' Body-parts

The fact that several of my sisters' body-parts
have had to be removed is irrelevant

but all I'm saying is it might explain,
or help explain, how come they rarely smile.

Compassion

They are rude – to anyone they feel like,
to those who are too fat, or too thin;

to Doris, to the cowman, to the cows,
but most of all to me but what the hell,

do I care about their cuticles?
About their hair? About their latest lash-plumper?

About their lacy large and small and medium-sized
balcony bras? The answer is *Not much.*

I only really care about myself
and my desire to exude compassion.

The Giant Rabbit

My sisters have decided, in their wisdom,
to move away to where I'll never visit them,

and all they have for company is money,
their neighbour's giant rabbit, and Jesus,

Who watches them feeding it with interest
as He Himself doesn't keep rabbits.

In Rooms That Echo Like Suburban Swimming-pools

I'm told they live on lettuces and fudge
in rooms that echo like suburban swimming-pools

in which they pray; in which they're losing it;
and when they hear my name I'm told they quail.

Shrimps

They live like shrimps crammed into a pot
and trying not to cry. The fact is

their only friend is Jesus Whose deep wounds
they dream they pack with spiders' webs and mosses.

The Tender Nurses

The tender nurses make them want to cry.
Everything makes them want to cry –

the doctor with a rabbit in his arms,
the snowflakes on his boots, the tender nurses,

the fact they're certain (but they're not *that* certain)
that they will meet their Maker when they die.

The Heavens

Men in aprons walk about with blankets
through rooms that are unlived in, like the heavens.

BEHOLD MY FATHER
ON HIS BICYCLE

Sure there have been injuries and deaths in boxing but none of them serious.

ALAN MINTER (former boxer)

Behold My Father in a Little Hat

Behold my father in a little hat
bicycling along down the lane;

behold him hide the bike in the hedge
and, having rolled his flannel trousers up,

behold my father paddle in the river
while savouring one of his mints.

My Father's Hands

His hands are like the hands of a statue
one knows one does not use for holding hands;

his nose is like the spout of the jug,
or would be if the spout had hairs inside it;

his cheeks are like the galvanised buckets
standing by the butts in the snow.

Lollipops

When a human hand or lip approaches
they fall apart in panic on their sticks

because they are afraid of being warm
and sliding down inside a sleeve like weasels.

Thunderflies

He hasn't spoken since we first set off
and all there is to do is count the thunderflies

dying or not dying on the windscreen
and hope the road will end before we get there.

The Party

If my father was a different man,
a man who was more gentle, say, or younger,

that man, too, would find it difficult
and so I shouldn't blame the one I've got –

or should I say the one that's got me,
whose party dress doesn't fool anybody.

The Finnish Word for Please

Is it true there's no such word as *can't*?
that no one knows the Finnish word for *please*?

that something bad is just about to happen
that even fathers can't protect you from?

Entomology

His suit is like a suit made of water
with buttons made of ice that whispers *love me*,

love me for myself and for the others
keenly crushing deadly laurel leaves.

Tarmac

As tarmac shimmers in the noonday heat
and unattended sprinklers spin on lawns,

he's stationed in the river like a bittern
that's seeing what it's like to be a man.

Chocolate Semolina

He's reading to the girl on the bed
as if the girl is me but she's not:

the girl I really am has gone away
to somewhere warm where tenderness makes sense

and blankets are as warm as melted chocolate
and chocolate sauce and chocolate semolina.

My Father's Hat

Because my father always wears a hat
I used to think he used to have a twin

who used to be conjoined at the head;
whose head was still half there inside the hat.

It Happens All the Time

It happens all the time. I clamber out,
turn my back, throw up, and on we go,

lay-by after lay-by, and the barley-sugar
he slides inside my cheek is worse than useless.

Anaesthesia

Is anyone afraid of anaesthesia?
Of men in flannel trousers? Starry nights?

Of living in a world where clothes that fit
never fit properly – except me?

My Father's Watch

When my father glances at his watch,
rises from his chair, and leaves the room

things that have been waiting to happen,
but never could happen, now can.

Boys in Shorts

Fathers, even mine, were once boys –
boys in shorts whose tiny minds the thought

of being someone's father never crossed,
least of all of a little girl.

Oscillating Sprinklers

He's never seen the oscillating sprinklers
spinning round on other people's lawns

and me, with all my clothes off, doing star-jumps;
or, if he has, it's none of his business.

Men Who Ride

Men who ride demand discreet admirers;
Afghan hounds demand boiled eggs;

tired boys demand chocolate pudding
and he, my father, *punctuality*.

The Hutch at the End of the Garden

As I watch him walk towards the hutch
I know it is about to begin –

the life I will be leading as an adult
who never wants to please him again.

Hope

If what we mean by hope is first hope
and then the pleasure of forgoing hope,

of waking up to find our hearts are broken
like broken snail-shells, then I hope.

Duct-tape

Duct-tape, duct-tape, duct-tape, what is duct-tape?
And what is fur and what is dressed wool

and is wool hair and why is duct-tape duct-tape
and are things basically good and basically workable

or are they not? And what about front crawl?
And fathers have warm coats and warm pyjamas

but do they have warm hearts? And does God care?
And does He even know? And does He know

that duct-tape cures veruccas? Does He know
that *duck-tape* sounds much better than duct-tape?

that how it sounds is not the point? that frankly
I believe He ought to know it is.

The Girl

This afternoon I found a dead girl
but when my father talked to me about her

what had been a quiet, private thing
between the girl and me became public.

My Father's Birthday

Everything about him seems to say
he knows he's just that little bit better –

the tie he wears, the tulips he arranges,
the presents he accepts without opening.

Violets

Violets are violet not blue;
women who are happy are naïve;

aviation fascinates murderers;
chainsaws were invented for the blind;

children need their fathers; laryngectomees
never say they want to go home.

Children Who Start Crying

Children who start crying should be gagged
and children who are gagged should be shot

and children who are kind are like pearls
nobody knows how to string.

Knots

A knot's not always like the kind of knot
I tie myself in knots in when I'm cross:

a knot can also be a small snipe,
an even-tempered and phlegmatic bird.

Aquaria

The man I never think of as my father
or as a man capable of grief

has never known the love of his daughter
because his daughter loves only fish.

Pebbles

Pebbles spend millions of years
smoothing and grooming each other

but he and I are humans and not pebbles
and humans haven't got that kind of time scale.

The Lake District

The Kendal Mint Cake tablets in his sock drawer
suggest a kind of untoward despair

I'm put off mint and sock drawers for life by
and nor will I return to the Lake District.

Mountaineers

Mountaineers attract guardian angels;
fishermen always have red hands;

rugby players look like floodlit mutton;
my father is a man of few words.

Swans

The glasses of the men who aren't my father
reflect the sparkling surface of the sea

where airbeds in the shape of hippopotami
are bumping into airbeds shaped like swans.

Antarctica

The lollipops, like saints, are staring down at me
as if they have been put there to remind me

what it is that is required of me;
like men who prey on bears in Antarctica.

Chess

Don't tell me what I should or shouldn't do;
don't look at me; don't wear, or spray, cologne;

don't say a single word against Kandinsky,
and never ever beat me at chess.

Everyone Likes Sex

Everyone likes sex, if only sometimes;
everyone likes whimbrels, and toast;

everyone likes distant snow-capped mountain-tops
and sharing flattering pictures of themselves,

and everyone likes fillies, and clean underwear,
but nobody likes to be bullied.

Heat

Why does he refuse to take his jacket off
even though he looks too hot to breathe?

Is nobody allowed to see his arms?
Are his arms private, like a morgue?

Is breathing in and out now private too?
And is it true that hatred isn't hatred

but love itself taken to extremes?
All I know for certain is the heat.

Cyclists

Cyclists who win prizes can't be trusted;
beef is sweet but not as sweet as horsemeat;

flame-retardants cling, or stick, to breast fat,
and fathers always do the best they can.

Sugar Lumps

In the hall hangs the long coat
in which he keeps a small supply of sugar lumps

that seem to me to have a slight air
of melancholy, like the sounds of jazz

I've only ever heard in the distance
on summer nights, as of adults dreaming.

Boxer Shorts

Traffic wardens sleep standing up;
anchovies discolour in warm cream;

confession isn't always enough
and boxer shorts are out of the question.

Ricky Hatton

Do I think he should have walked away
from what must be the least forgiving sport?

And do I think nude modelling is demeaning?
And how can someone generate trust

in someone who's as proud as an orange
that does not need a squeezer or a duck;

who, seeking to inspire the awe in children
that cattle have for cattle-grids, will lie?

Boys on Bicycles

Although the boys on bicycles, in swimming-trunks,
bicycling to and from the rocks,

know it's true I'm not allowed to swim there,
in swimwear I am not allowed to wear,

they do not know that on the day I do
I swim until I meet only fish.

My Father's Friends

I usually disown him if I can.
He doesn't look the part so it's easy –

silver hair, a truss, and no contemporaries
to call his friends. Alas, he has no friends.

Swimwear

Waiting on the rocks in the rain
to jump the jump I'm not allowed to jump,

I tell myself, in order to empower myself,
there's nothing I don't know about swimwear.

Strawberries

Maybe *someone else* is my enemy
and not my father and I've got it wrong –

or maybe it's *as well as* my father,
like when you get suckers of something,

suckers or runners, like strawberries
blindly smothering a bank.

The Feel of Noughts

(for László Krasznahorkai)

I hate the size and smell of hotel lobbies,
(why can't people simply stay at home?)

I hate the noughts that look and feel like zeros;
the sheep that look like shit; the tall buildings;

I hate the fact I can't pronounce his name –
and the worrying thought that happiness might be selfish.

Golf

He glares at me like owls; or like the golfer
who can't not play according to strict rules;

who wakes to find something in his coffee
that may or may not be some kind of worm.

Greyhounds

Do fathers always love their own children?
And did he once love me? And when he touches me

does he think he can't hold out much longer
against the thoughts it pains him not to think

that race across his brain like hairless greyhounds
across a world exempt from love and sin.

Starry Nights

My father wakes me up on starry nights
and takes me out to wonder at the stars

that couldn't give a shit about the names
my father so triumphantly assigns to them.

The King

Nothing moves except the winding river
and dragonflies that only move to stop

and, on the bank, my father, like a king
who can't remember over whom he's ruling.

Carp

Are goldfish ever sad? And can ghosts swim?
And yes, there's more to life than breeding goldfish

but can you tell me what? Breeding carp?
Breeding carp so big they can't move

and live and die in specially-built aquaria
where teams of virgins feed each one by hand?

The Nurse

Loved not for herself but for her breasts,
she dreams she's not a nurse but a bicycle,

elegant, efficient and amusing,
with spokes that can be made to play a tune.

Acrobatics

On this final sweltering afternoon
I don't know which of us is more unlikeable –

me in skin-tight shorts and little else
performing one of my death-defying somersaults

or him, my father, in his mackintosh,
gazing not at me but at the thunder-clouds

as if to say I may be upside-down
but he himself is *bound for Eternity*.

Periwinkle Blue

Can we really die of broken hearts
like Jubilee and Circle Line mosquitoes

dying for the sunshine of the Nile?
And can you tell me how a dying man,

or if a dying man, serves a purpose?
And did you whisper periwinkle blue?

Periwinkle blue? You must be joking!
Whose face was ever *periwinkle blue*?

Kandinsky

Everybody's running up and down,
sobbing as they run, except Kandinsky,

a fish so cool he knows he's going to die
but lives as if he doesn't in the meantime.

The Coffee Drinker

Made by God to drink only coffee
(and God, like mathematics, can't be wrong)

my father is now living in Eternity
where there is neither coffee nor tea.

The Maid

Like a little maid who's so dim-witted
she doesn't understand she is alone

but carries on working as before,
I carry on, alone in his fine castle.

Keeper of My Bath

The spider who is keeper of my bath
likes to take her time as if to say

self-discipline is in a way self-discipline
and in a way effortless chic.

ACKNOWLEDGEMENTS

I would like to than *The Moth, The London Review of Books, The Poetry Review* and *The Times Literary Supplement* in whose pages some of these poems first appeared.

I would also like to thank Penny Dunscombe, of Cloak and Dagger, for help with printing, Rod Hill and Sidekick for help with lifts; Phoebe and Rose for help with texting; Ann Gray for the giraffe and Cai for the postcards.

I would also like to thank Lorraine Knowles, Julie McFeeters, Barbara Preston and Elaine Summers at Lyme Regis Library for their enviable good humour and efficiency.

And of course I would like to thank Neil Astley whose feathers it's impossible to ruffle.

MIX
Paper from
responsible sources
FSC® C007785
FSC
www.fsc.org